Silent Tower

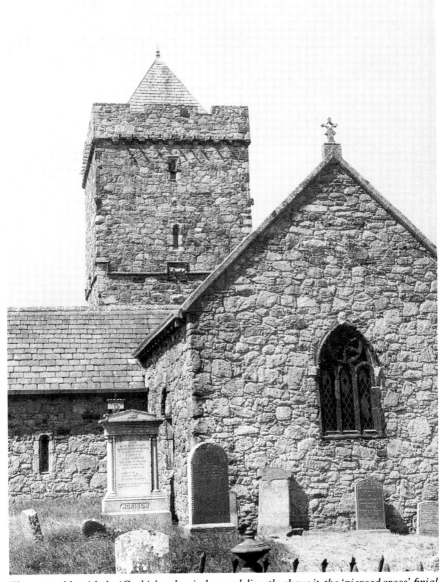

The east gable with the 'Gothic' style window and directly above it, the 'pierced cross' finial. The tower is at the west end, and the south transept to the left. The larger tombstone, close to the south wall, is that of the well known Harris blacksmith and evangelist, John Morison (Ian, Gobha na Hearadh).

Silent Tower

A History and Description of St. Clements
Church at Rodil

by

John M. MacAulay

The Pentland Press Limited
Edinburgh · Cambridge · Durham

First published in 1993 by
The Pentland Press Ltd.
1 Hutton Close
South Church
Bishop Auckland
Durham

ISBN 1 85821 038 0

Typeset by Elite Typesetting Techniques, Southampton.
Printed and bound by Antony Rowe Ltd., Chippenham.

To my wife,
Cathy

Contents

Acknowledgements

I gratefully acknowledge the assistance of the following, for their help with gathering information, and for permission for using certain items relating to St. Clement's Church:

The Royal Commission on the Ancient and Historical Monuments of Scotland.
The National Museums of Scotland.
National Register of Archives.
Museum nan Eilean.
Leabharlann nan Eilean.
The Right Honourable Anne, Countess of Dunmore.
Norman Jr. Macmillan.
Sig. Guiseppe Caruso.
D. Eugenio Andrea Gargiulo.
Revd David F. Huie.
Historic Scotland.
Special thanks to Chrissie Macleod of Kintulavig, for her first reading of the manuscript; and to the Macdonald family of RODIL CROFTING LANDS my heartfelt appreciation for their encouragement and assistance. The publication of this book has been sponsored by Western Isles Enterprise and the LEADER Programme.

John MacAulay.

Introduction

My interest in the ancient church of St. Clement's at Rodil arose out of the lack of information available on its history and architecture, coupled with the fact that most local people who had any knowledge and interest in its past history have long since passed from the scene of time. An immense amount of valuable historical information has disappeared with them, as a lot of past events were not documented, but passed on orally. The little that now remains has been watered down over the centuries to what is now only an indistinct flavour of what had been an extremely powerful heritage of religious history and practices, Clan Macleod history and traditions, and many more stories of illustrious people and important events that were woven into the mysterious tapestry of time.

It is sad that a noble building, which still stands complete and in an excellent state of repair, has no complete record of its history available, not only for the many visitors who come from all parts of the world, but also for those who are solely interested in churches and other similar buildings; and the people of Harris, for whom St. Clement's is a valuable part of their heritage, who would also benefit from a written account of its past.

My own knowledge was, to say the least, scant; but the urge to gather any information that was available grew until I had collected what I hope will be of interest to others, thereby stimulating renewed concern for our past. I make no claim of attempting to create a true historical document, but only of gathering what little is available from written reports, local history and folklore – and presenting it to the reader in such a way as to paint a picture of the life of the building and glimpses of the people who, by reason of their birth, upbringing, deeds or misdeeds, grew into the stones of St. Clement's church.

Eighteenth century Rodil: showing Rodil House and the harbour built by Captain Alexander Macleod. St. Clement's church is on the hill to the right.

To avoid any confusion with differences in the various spellings of the place names, I shall use the older form of spelling: Rodil, in preference to the modern Rodel, since the name occurs as Rodil in most older references. The Gaelic form of the name is *Roghadal*, probably derived from the Norse words *raudr* and *dalr* meaning 'red dale', which reflects the nature of the soil in that area.

In collecting and assembling the fragments of evidence to its eventful past, and particularly where there had been previously speculation and guesswork in dating the origin of the building, I have come to some conclusions of my own. The same applies to previously contested aspects of its construction.

It is generally believed that Alasdair Crotach was responsible for the building of the church, from the ruins of a previous building, though all evidence suggests that he only repaired or restored it. In the *Statistical Account* of 1792, the Revd John Macleod of the parish of Harris, at Scarista, suggests its origins dated from the flourishing times of 'Icolmkill'

St. Clement's church from the south-east, with Sranndabhal to the left of the tower; the western shoulder of Roineabhal – at 460 metres above sea level, the highest hill in South Harris – is to the right. Just visible below Roineabhal is part of the crofting township of Rodil.

– St. Columba's Iona – to which all the lands of Harris are said to have once belonged. That there had been another building at or very near to the same site previously, I have no doubt, though there is no trace of it now – its materials were probably used in later repairs, or removed and used elsewhere. This other building was the Augustinian priory which existed up to the time of the Reformation, and which I now believe to have stood along with St. Clement's church for a period of around two hundred years.

It has been suggested by some that the tower on the west end had been built in stages over a period of time, but it is more likely to have been planned and built as a complete structure. The divisions on the outer walls of the tower, formed by the black stringing, are purely ornamental; and there is absolutely no indication on the internal masonry of the tower that it had been built in stages. I have no expert knowledge of architecture, and here again I am attempting to create what can only be a general picture within my own limitations. There were skilled craftsmen employed on the construction of the church and tower; the fact that it still stands today, despite its turbulent past, and exposure to the elements, bears testimony to their ability.

The skill of the sculptors who executed the various carvings and ornamentation, inside and outside the church, was of a very high order, and we must bear in mind that those carvings have been exposed to the weather, also to fire on more than one occasion, and goodness only knows what other rough treatment over the years that have passed since the hand of the sculptor left them perfectly finished and finely detailed.

There are still long periods of time that I cannot account for at present, but I would like to think that, sometime, those parts of the picture will reappear from somewhere and help to enlarge the view we now have.

I have made no attempt to go into the complex history of the Macleod chiefs in their connection with St. Clement's, as this is in itself a specialised subject and is also already fairly well documented. I have only tried to fit in those names and dates that tie in with the history of St. Clement's church.

In the course of my research I came across a reference to some relics having been shipped to Rome in the ninth century, for protection from the Norse invaders; also a beggar's badge, made from lead, has been mentioned, which ties in with records of poor people in the parish of Harris (1792 *Statistical Account*). The only other known relic is a small brass chalice that was found in the churchyard.

As to the history of St. Clement's church as a place of worship, there are no records, but it appears to have been used only sporadically, and not for any long periods of time. It certainly has not been in use in recent times, except for the occasional marriage or baptism. After the restoration by Catherine, Countess of Dunmore in 1873, the interior of the church had not been furnished; there was no seating or pulpit installed. Shortly after this time, in 1895, the kirk session for the parish of Harris made enquiries as to its past use, and the possibility of bringing it under the jurisdiction of the established church in Scotland as a regular place of worship. This did not take place, and the church has lain empty and unused since that time. When the church was restored by Captain Alexander Macleod in 1784-87 it was completely and, most likely, very elaborately furnished, but its use must have been very limited for shortly after, in 1792, the Revd John Macleod of the parish of Harris, who wrote the Harris report for the *Statistical Account*, mentions its use only for occasional divine service.

Going back to Alasdair Crotach's time, it is likely to have been for the sole benefit of the chief and his followers, for private worship, marriages, funerals, etc.; as this was about the time of the Reformation, the religious state of the island people must have been very unstable. Prior to the Reformation it would have undoubtedly been under the control of the Augustinian priory.

I feel that since Alasdair Crotach's time St. Clement's church became mainly a status symbol – powerhouse of the Macleod chiefs – and this feeling is reflected locally in that St. Clement's is seldom referred to as a church, but is more commonly called 'the tower'.

To those that helped me in my search for pieces of information, I offer my sincere thanks; and my apologies to anyone inadvertently missed out from the list of acknowledgements. Every scrap of what may have seemed to be of doubtful value has had its place – sometimes only one word or a date would help to bring previously unrelated parts together.

John M. MacAulay

Significant dates
in the history of St. Clement's church.

563 AD	St. Columba lands in Iona.
565	Columba's mission to the Isles.
8th-13th century	Culdees in Scotland.
794	Beginning of the Norse invasion of Scotland.
8th-15th century	Norse occupation of the Hebrides.
1098	Magnus 'Bareleg' claims the Western Isles.
1100	Augustinians come to Britain.
1266	Western Isles annexed by the Crown.
1480	Battle of Bloody Bay, near Tobermory.
1517	Reformation in Europe.
1528	Restoration of St. Clement's by Alasdair Crotach.
1546	Alasdair Crotach dies.
1739	*Long nan Daoine* – the *William* of Donaghadee.
1779	Harris purchased by Captain Alexander Macleod.
1784	1st restoration by Captain Alexander Macleod.
1789	2nd restoration by Captain Alexander Macleod.
1792	*Statistical Account.*
1873	Restoration by Catherine, Countess of Dunmore.
1928	RCAHMS report.

1

The Hebrides

The Heboudai of Ptolemy; the Hebudes of Pliny; or the Western Isles of Scotland. Of the five hundred and twenty or so islands off the west coast of Scotland, the group known as the Western Isles are separated from the mainland by the North and South Minches and the Sea of the Hebrides, varying in distance from approximately forty miles to about twelve miles at the narrowest part. The shortest ferry crossing is from Uig on the Isle of Skye to Tarbert in Harris – a distance of twenty-five miles.

The islands run in a north-east to south-west direction over a distance of one hundred and thirty miles, from the Butt of Lewis at the north end to Barra Head at the southern extremity. Born of the oldest rock in the world, the islands are on the whole quite mountainous, though not of any significant height. The tallest is the Clisham on north Harris – 799 metres above sea level. The lower ground is blanketed with peat, reaching a depth of eight metres in places: the only indigenous source of fuel for the islanders. Other areas of glacier-worn granite resemble a barren moonscape. The rugged coastline is indented with numerous bays and sea lochs; the Atlantic coast on the western side of the islands is relieved by magnificent stretches of golden shell sands which, when blown inland by the winter storms, help to sweeten the acid peatland, resulting in a very fertile soil – *machair* land – good grazing for sheep and cattle, but probably better known for the spring and summer displays of wild flowers. The islands are a haven for wildlife and especially noted for the large colonies of seabirds feeding on the rich fisheries of the Atlantic – fisheries sadly being depleted for commercial gain, and mainly by vessels from outwith the islands.

At one time, crofting was the mainstay of island life: a form of agriculture where individuals occupied small areas of arable land, with rough

1

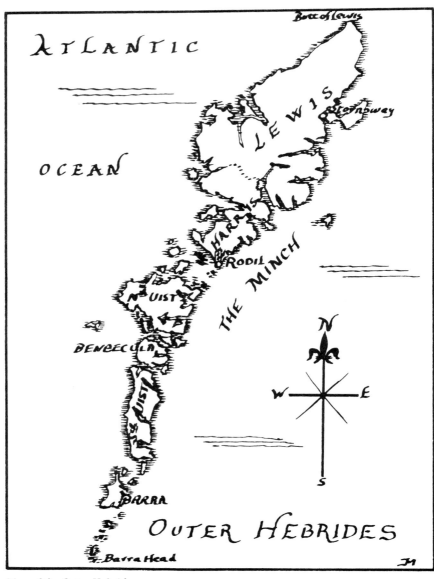

Map of the Outer Hebrides.

pasture held in common. It gives a precarious existence, as a croft does not provide sufficient income to support a family, with the result that crofting has become secondary to some other form of employment: maybe fishing or fish farming; weaving Harris Tweed; or in the construction industry. Catering for tourists during the short summer season provides a welcome source of income for some housewives.

The Hebrides were colonised by the Norsemen from the ninth to the thirteenth century, and to this day most of the principal place names: islands; hills; lochs; settlements and townships, are of Norse origin. The Western Isles Islands Council (*Comhairle nan Eilean*) is responsible for local government. It is a single tier authority, centred in Stornoway, on the Isle of Lewis: a forward looking body, which has made a valuable contribution to the improvement of social and environmental conditions on the islands.

2

Early Forms of Religion

Near to the central point of the Outer Hebrides, close by the Sound of Harris where the waters of the Minch are twice daily fed by the mighty Atlantic Ocean, lies the small crofting township of Rodil, site of the ancient church of St. Clement – reputed to be one of the earliest church buildings in the whole of Scotland.

It is not known for certain who this particular St. Clement was, but he is generally thought to be the Clement referred to by the apostle Paul in his epistle to the Philippians – in chapter 4 and at verse 3: 'With Clement also and with other of my fellow labourers, whose names are in the book of life.'

It could also have been Titus Flavius Clemens, more commonly known as Clement of Alexandria: one of the most famous teachers of the Christian church in the second and third centuries. He was regarded as a saint until he was struck off the calendar by Benedict XIV. His works included the *Proptreptikos*, *Paidagogos* and *Stromateis* – the first, an exhortation to the Greeks to turn to the one and true God; the second, a work on Christ; and the last, some discursions in chronology, philosophy and poetry.

Another possible candidate is Clemens Romanus (Clement of Rome) first of numerous Popes named Clement. He is credited with writing an epistle to the Corinthians.

St. Clement, who is also regarded as the patron saint of boatmen, ferrymen and fishermen, has associated with him as patron or protector, a symbol – an anchor – but strangely, this is not to be found among the numerous other marks at Rodil.

The story is told that Clement suffered death by being cast into the sea, with an anchor attached to his body. But by a Divine command, the sea

4

receded for a distance of three miles at the place of his drowning; and the strange sight of the holy man enshrined in a little temple was witnessed by wondering beholders. This miraculous phenomenon occurred each year on the anniversary of his death – a circumstance which permitted pilgrimage to the sacred spot. In ecclesiastical art, the anchor is employed as a symbol of the saint, and his votaries are the children of the sea. St. Clement's festival day is 23 November, commemorating the anniversary of his martyrdom which, it is related, took place probably in the first century of the Christian era.

> And we shall give the glory
> To the Trinity and Clement
> And the great clerk who lies at Rodil

– from the 'Sea Hymn of Dunvegan'.

The early history of the church is somewhat obscure. The Revd J.M. Wilson in his *Gazetteer of Scotland* says of it: 'The churches [of the islands] together with the smaller chapels, all seem to have depended immediately on the monastry of Rodil, dedicated to St. Clement, which, though its foundation is attributed to David I (Scotland's Sore Saint) is generally supposed to be of more ancient date.' Canon R.C. Macleod of Macleod (Macleods of Dunvegan) states: 'Whatever the earlier history of the monastry may have been, it belonged to the Augustinian Canons at the end of the twelfth century.' This Augustinian priory, one of about twenty-five similar ones throughout Scotland, was established at Rodil in the twelfth century by the Canons Regular of St. Augustine, or Austin Canons, who were introduced into Britain and established themselves at Scone in 1114. They were followers of the teachings of St. Augustine, who was born in AD 354, a renowned father of the Christian church; he wrote on the doctrines of free-will and grace, his greatest work being *De Civitate Dei* (City of God). He died on 28 August 430 AD. The Augustinian followers took vows of chastity and poverty. There was also an order of nuns of the same name.

This priory had been built on or near the site of an ancient Culdee cell – very early Christian – which itself was founded on a pre-Christian Druid temple which had existed from primeval times, dedicated to the worship of the sun. Some aspects of this sun-worship were evident as late as the nineteenth century, when the corpse of the dead was carried three times sun-wise round St. Clement's church. Every physical undertaking by the

Druids – Gaelic *Draoi*, meaning magicians – was sun-wise or *deiseal*. There are other Druid sites throughout the island: notably, the standing stones at Nisabost and Borve. Many suns have set over those stones since the Druid priests set them up. There is very little known about the Druid sun-worshippers whose idolatry prevailed from early times, except that as priests they possessed a considerable share of civil power and were highly esteemed by the common people; they had some knowledge of geometry – indicated by their precise placing of stones in relation to the sun and stars; they dabbled in magic, and surrounded themselves with mysteries that fenced them from the ordinary people. There is no visible evidence of their existence at Rodil; the Culdees who came later could have destroyed or used for some other purpose any stone edifice they may have constructed. They were finally driven from Scotland by King Cratalinth about the year 277 AD.

Only from this time can we, with any degree of certainty, date the true era of Christianity in Scotland. A church was built by Cratalinth in Iona as a place of refuge for both preachers and professors from the southern parts of Britain who were suffering persecution under Emperor Dioclesian, in the beginning of the fourth century. It is not known for certain if those refugees were the ancient Culdees, or a different set of believers.

The Culdees (from *Cultores Dei*, worshippers of God) flourished during the reign of Cratalinth, and his successor Fincormac, but later fell into disorder following the death of the latter. They were driven from mainland Scotland into Ireland and the western isles of Denmark and Norway, in 380 AD, after the battle of Dunne in Carrick. It is possible for some to have wandered in the Hebrides during this time; around 420 AD, however, the Culdees were recalled from their lurking-places and returned to their churches, where they were held in greater esteem than ever before. Many were later amalgamated with the Roman Church in Scotland, but some stood out on their own in opposition to this form of worship: notably Clements and Samson, the two most famous in the seventh century for upholding the gospel of Christ. It is interesting to note the name Clements in connection with the Culdees, but it is doubtful if this had anything to do with the name of the church at Rodil. The Culdees transmitted their testimony to the Lollards – a society founded in Antwerp (1300 AD) for the care of the sick and the burial of the dead, represented in this country by the followers of Wycliffe, many of whom were put to death during the reign of Henry V. The Lollards did much in England to pave the way for the Reformation.

According to W.F. Skene's *Celtic Scotland*, they 'originally sprang from that ascetic order who adopted a solitary service of God in an isolated cell as the highest form of religious life and who were termed '*Deicoloe*': that they then became associated in communities of anchorites, or hermits; that they were clerics, and might be called monks, but only in the sense of which anchorites were monks.'

Close to St. Clement's church there is a hillock named *Cnoc nan Croisean*, (Hill of Crosses) where the Culdee missionaries would have raised their crosses and preached in the open air, especially at the times of Druid ceremonies, gradually winning over to Christianity the followers of the Druids.

There were many other temples and religious sites in the islands, maybe as many as a dozen on Harris alone: for example, one dedicated to St. Taranus, from which the island of Taransay is named; St. Bride's or Brigit's at Scarista, site of the present Church of Scotland. The parish of Harris, centred on Scarista, formerly known as the parish of Kilbride, is on record as having the first minister, a Malcolm Macpherson, who was granted parsonage and vicarage of St. Bride for life in 1566, by the Earl of Argyll, and confirmed by Queen Mary in 1567. The name Kilbride has all but disappeared from the map of Harris today, existing only in the name of an offshore rock, *Bo na Cille*. Totally submerged in over three fathoms of water, its position is only betrayed by the Atlantic swell bursting over it before finally expending its energy on the two-mile stretch of golden sand below the church.

The sites of twelve ancient chapels could still be identified as late as 1792, but little remains today that is recognisable. Any religious documents or records that existed may have been hidden or destroyed at the time of the Reformation: that religious upheaval in the sixteenth century which changed the face of Europe. The leaders of the movement were aiming to reform the church after the corruption of mediaeval Romanism, with emphasis on a pure form of Christianity as represented in the New Testament. It was revival on a grand scale. The revolt by Luther, a German monk, began in 1517 and, with the help of John Calvin, spread throughout Europe and Scandinavia. In Scotland, the teaching of Calvin was followed, even to the extent of turning against the throne – an advance not only in religion but, at that time, in civilisation.

It is interesting to note that years later, the fear of Roman Catholicism becoming re-established through the influence of 'Bonnie Prince Charlie' spurred the Revd John Macaulay, Presbyterian minister of South Uist, into action, when he heard the Prince had landed at Rossinish – on the run after Culloden in April 1746. The Revd Macaulay, the grandfather of Lord Macaulay, the noted historian and politician who is buried at Westminster Abbey, sent word to his father, the Revd Aulay Macaulay, minister of the parish of Harris at Scarista, to inform Lord Fortrose's factor at Stornoway of his presence and to take steps to seize him. This failed, and the Prince, not without great difficulty, was spirited away.

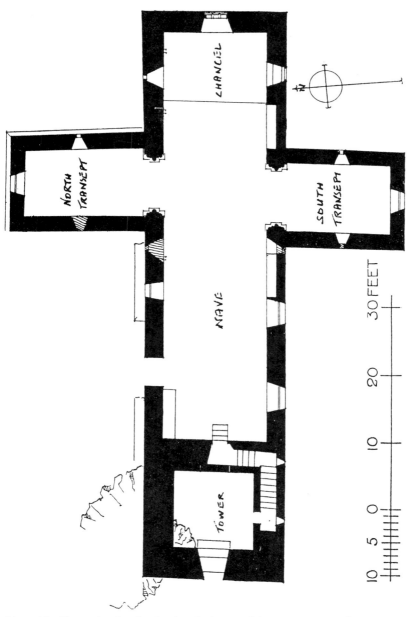

Plan of St. Clement's church, showing the layout of the tower, nave and transepts.

3

A Brief History of the Church Building

The origin of St Clement's church, as we know it today, is not possible to be dated with any degree of accuracy; but it could have been built by the first Macleod chief of Harris, Tormod, whose father Leod (son of Olave the Black – a Kinglet of Man) had rule over Lewis and Harris in the thirteenth century. The two sons, Torquil and Tormod, at the time of his death, were given the lands of Lewis and Harris respectively. This could date the building as very early fourteenth century, considering that we know it was in need of repair about two hundred years later; that work was implemented by Alasdair Crotach, 8th chief of the Macleods of Harris and Dunvegan. It is said that Torquil was responsible for the building of St. Columba's church at Uidh (Eye) near Stornoway (burial place of the Macleods of Lewis) of which only the ruined walls are standing today.

That St. Clement's church suffered at the time of the Reformation is certain; a marble plaque inscribed in Latin gives evidence of this. An adjoining convent of friars and nuns is referred to, but there is no trace of this to be found. The plaque, translated, reads as follows:

This sacred edifice, the very walls of
which had been scarcely spared through
the fury attendant upon religious change,
which in its universal pillage devastated
everything, and levelling the adjoining
convent of friars and nuns to the ground,
consecrate to the piety of his ancestors in
former times to God and St. Clement, after
having been for now over two hundred years
roofless and neglected, was repaired and

A view along the south wall of the nave; at the far end is the doorway leading upwards into the tower.

adorned, and after having been accidentally
destroyed by fire, was restored a second
time by Alexander Macleod of Herries in
1787 AD.

During this restoration which was begun in 1784, the building was roofed
and slated; the interior was in the process of being furnished, at great cost,
for which all the necessary materials were stored inside the church. Ow-
ing to carelessness by the carpenters, a fire was left unattended, which
ignited some wood shavings during the night and set fire to the whole
building. Again at Alexander Macleod's own expense, it was re-roofed
and repaired – but was left unfinished at the time of his death.

For some time after this, the church was used as one of the principal
places in the parish for celebrating Divine service. It is recorded in the
minutes of the synod of Argyll that a John Campbell was minister of St.
Clement's in 1670, and also held Barra as part of his parish. This John
Campbell was actually minister of the parish of Harris (then known as the
parish of Kilbride), based at Scarista. It is quite likely that his services
were called upon to preach at Rodil; possibly this was the only time in the
whole history of St. Clement's that it was in regular use for Protestant
worship.

Alasdair Crotach (the hunch-back) Macleod, chief of the Macleods of
Harris and Dunvegan, had previously carried out restoration work in the
early sixteenth century, probably the first major repairs to be done to the
church. Alasdair Crotach – whose deformity was due to a sword wound
which had severed muscles in the back of his neck around the time of the
battle of Bloody Bay – had his tomb built in St. Clement's church. It is a
masterpiece of design and sculpture, regarded as one of the finest in
Scotland. It is dated 1528 – eighteen years before he died. One cannot
help but wonder if he himself had a part in the design of his own tomb, to
have it built into the restored church; or could this have been the church's
way of recognising his services? Alasdair Crotach died in 1546 and was
laid to rest in the burial place of his ancestors – Rodil – the 'Westminster
of the isles'. One of the sculptured panels on his tomb reads:

> This tomb was erected by Alexander,
> son of William Macleod, Lord of
> Dunvegan, anno domini 1528

A more detailed description of this remarkable tomb is given in Chapter 6.

4

Faces and Places

The 'Alexander Macleod of Herries' who was responsible for the restoration work in 1787 was Captain Alexander Macleod, who had command of the East-Indiaman *Mansfield*. He purchased the estate of Harris and St. Kilda in 1779, from the trustees of his relative Lieutenant General Norman Macleod of Macleod, for the sum of £16,000. In addition to this work on St. Clement's church, he was also responsible for the building of a new church at Scarista: a building of stone and lime with a slated roof, to replace the previous church with its thatched roof on this site, which had been destroyed by fire. The Revd John Macleod, whose report on the parish of Harris appears in the *Statistical Account* of 1792, was himself admitted to this charge in the same year the new church was completed.

In the churchyard at Rodil is a *caibeal* (burial chapel) erected by Captain Macleod, with a plaque to his father's memory, inscribed as follows:

To the memory of Donald Macleod of
Berneray, son of John, tutor of Macleod
who in vigour of body and mind and
firm adherence to the principals of
his ancestors, resembled the men of
former times. His grandfather and
granduncle were knighted by Charles
II for their loyalty and distinguished
valour in the Battle of Worcester.
When the standard of the House of
Stuart, to which he was attached,
was displayed A.D. 1745, though past
the prime of life, he took up arms,

had a share in the action of that
period and in the Battle of Falkirk
vanquished a dragoon hand to hand.
From this time he lived at his house
in Berneray, universally beloved and
respected. In his 75th year he
married his third wife by whom he
had nine children, and died in his
90th year, 16th December, 1783. This
monument was erected by his son
Alexander Macleod of Herries esq.

Donald Macleod, at the age of 75, had to prove his physical ability before
getting married for the third time, by performing *Leum a bhradain* (the
salmon leap). This was done by lying flat on his back on the floor, and
from that position, propelling himself with a powerful jerk of his body, up
onto the bed.

His third wife was sixteen-year-old Margaret Macleod, daughter of the
Revd Donald Macleod of Greshornish; their family of nine were as follows:

Captain Donald Macleod
Lieutenant-General Sir John Macleod, KCB
Captain Alexander Macleod (of Herries)
Lieutenant-General Sir Charles Macleod, KCB
Alexandrina, who married Norman Macleod, of Drynoch
Anne, who married Kenneth Campbell, of Strond
Marion, who married Major Alexander Macleod, of Dalvey
Jessie, who married John Maclean, of Boreray
Christina, who married Major Macdonald, of Askernish
There was also a daughter who died in infancy

There is no indication as to where Captain Alexander Macleod is buried,
but there are several tombs from which the name plaque is missing,
having either been broken, or else removed at some time.

Exactly what terrible misfortunes befell the church of St. Clement's and
the neighbouring occupants of the priory during the invasion and subse-
quent occupation of the Hebrides by the *Tuadhroinnich* (Norsemen),
between the eighth and fifteenth centuries, is not known; though no doubt
they would not have escaped the rule of fire and sword. In the year 795,

Iona was ravaged by the Vikings, and in 802 the Columban monastry was burned down. This all happened before the reign of King Olaf (Tryggvason) of Norway (from 997 till his death in 1000 AD). Olaf was the first Christian King of Norway – though his method of dealing with non-believers would be regarded as very un-Christian today. Around this time, some religious relics from the priory were removed and shipped to Rome for safe keeping; possibly other less valuable artefacts would have been buried locally.

The Norsemen certainly left us a lasting reminder of their presence, in that the majority of principal place names throughout the islands: townships, settlements, hills, lochs and rivers, coastal rocks and islets are derived from the Norse language. Harris itself, for example, takes its name from the Norse, though there is confusion and uncertainty as to the actual meaning of it. Even the Gaelic form *na Hearadh* is not correct, as no Gaelic noun begins with 'h'. A more accurate spelling would be *na h-Earadh*. This does not really make sense either from a Gaelic point of view as it implies Easting. The closest Norse equivalent to *Hearadh*, is the word *horgr* meaning a heathen place of worship. This is a possibility considering the ancient history of Rodil which, even in Norse times, would have been the principal settlement on Harris.

It is remarkable that the church building has survived at all after suffering for hundreds of years from strife, fire, exposure to the harsh climate of the Outer Hebrides and plundering and abuse at various times, and although very little exists in the way of historical record, some stories have been handed down orally through the ages: colourful gems in an otherwise dark history.

A granddaughter of Alasdair Crotach, Mary Macleod, is reputed to have graced the court of Mary, Queen of Scots, and to have composed the ballad 'The Queen's Maries':

> Last night there were four Maries
> Tonight there be but three.
> There was Mary Beaton and Mary Seaton,
> And Mary Carmichael and me.

Mary Macleod eventually married a clan Macneil chieftain of Barra.

Underneath the floor of the church, and directly below the window in the south transept, lie the remains of another Mary Macleod – Mairi, *nighean Alasdair ruaidh* – bardess to the Macleods of Harris and Dunvegan. There is not a great deal known about the bardess: born in

1569 on the Isle of Harris, her father was Alasdair Macleod, son of
Alasdair *ruadh*, and very closely connected to the *siol Thormoid*
bloodline. Mairi spent her early years at Dunvegan as nurse or nanny to
the Macleod household, and it was to be much later in life that her talent
as a bardess was revealed. She composed many songs and poems in praise
of the Macleods, who were very close to her heart.

Free from the fetters of ancient bardic tradition, Mairi developed her
own enlightened style of expressing, in melodious words, her thoughts
and feelings towards this noble family. Lavish in her praise and liberal in
detail of life and the pleasures of extravagant pursuits at Dunvegan Castle, she also revealed to the world at large what could best be described as
mischievous gossip. Mairi was eventually banished to the Isle of Mull.

It has been said it is impossible to bridle a bard or a woman; Mairi was
both, and in her exile she found a new strength. She composed her best
known song '*Luinneag Mhicleoid*', a powerful composition guaranteed to
mellow the heart that banished her and kept her away from her beloved
Dunvegan. Macleod relented, and Mairi returned: on condition she re-
frained from expressing herself as before.

Mairi *nighean Alasdair ruaidh* died at Dunvegan Castle in 1674. She
had attained the grand old age of one hundred and five years. Her remains
were ferried across the Minch in Macleod's *Birlinn* to be interred at St.
Clement's church. As it was not always the truth that was portrayed in her
poetry, but often vain and arrogant flattery, Mairi asked to be buried face
downwards when she died, so that her lying tongue could not point to
Heaven. A later poet spoke more sympathetically of her:

> Not on the clouds would my eyes be,
> o' kinsfolk,
> But on Rodil of Harris.

Many chiefs of the Macleods of Harris and Dunvegan lie buried be-
neath the floor of St. Clement's church, as well as their standard-bearers.
Also laid to rest here are the famous MacCrimmons – hereditary pipers to
the Macleods – said to have come from Strond, though it is more likely
that they resided there whenever the chief was in Harris. The township of
Strond lies within sight of St. Clement's.

Other notable characters, now lost to time and memory, were buried at
Rodil. One of those later worthies was John Morison – *Ian, Gobha na
Hearadh* – born at Rodil in 1790; a blacksmith to trade, he later became a
catechist or evangelist, and composer of many fine hymns and poems. He

Harris stonemasons, Kenneth Macsween from Strond, and Donald MacAulay from Geocrab.
Fine examples of Highland manhood. Both men are buried at Rodil.

founded the Manish parish of the Free Church of Scotland in 1849, still in regular use today by the Church of Scotland. John Morison died in 1852, and his grave lies close to the south wall of St. Clement's church.

My own paternal grandparents and great-grandparents lie in a grave marked with a stone erected by Donald MacAulay – a great-granduncle; he was a stonemason to trade, and along with a fellow craftsman, Kenneth MacSween of Strond, travelled throughout Scotland in pursuit of his craft. A portrait of them both, in full Highland dress, is held by Museum nan Eilean at Stornoway. They were regarded as being very fine examples of Highland manhood at the time. They were both involved in the building of the castle at *Amhuinnsuidhe* – built for the Earl of Dunmore in 1868 – home to the Countess of Dunmore, who restored the church of St. Clement's, thereby creating further employment for the craftsmen who had now completed work on the castle.

The burial ground, which has been in use up to fairly recent times, is now closed.

5

The Church and its Architecture

The church, which is featured on most of the ancient maps and charts of the Hebrides, would have been a prominent landmark for mariners and travellers of that time. It is a solid, well constructed building, with the main walls approximately 2 feet 9 inches thick, built from local gneiss, laid in random fashion. Seven hundred years of exposure have had little effect on this hard and durable stone – reputed to be from some of the earliest formed rocks in the world. It is extremely difficult to work and shape using ordinary hand tools, and must have presented quite a problem for the masons, who were probably more used to working in freestone and similar sympathetic materials.

There is no doubting the skill of those masons, as there is a regularity to the basic stonework that is carried throughout the whole building. The finer carvings and mouldings were produced from a fine yellowish-green sandstone and black amphibolite. The sandstone was shipped from the same quarries at Carsaig on the Isle of Mull where the stone for the abbey on Iona was quarried. The amphibolite, or hornblende-schist, is obtainable locally, where it occurs sandwiched between layers of gneiss. A jet black stone, it is particularly attractive when wet, as it sparkles in the sunlight. The quality of the carved stonework must have been absolutely perfect; once again we must give consideration to the many years and long exposure to the elements that have not been so kind to this comparatively less durable stone, but from what we see today, we can still appreciate the excellent workmanship.

The finest external feature of the building is, without doubt, the east window. Carved from black amphibolite, it is of typical fourteenth century 'decorated Gothic' design, with projecting dripstone, terminating in carved head supports on each side. There are three vertical lights with

St. Clement's from the south, with Roineabhal in the background.

trefoil heads, surmounted by a six-spoked wheel within the arch. The remaining windows are of a simpler design with a single light; some are of lancet pattern.

The square tower at the west end of the church gives the whole structure a feeling of solidity, its four walls richly adorned with fine carvings and sculpted stone features. The black amphibolite band of cable-stringing, approximately half-way up the tower, has given some people the impression that it was built in stages, with the upper half added at a later date. There is no evidence to support this theory, the stringing being a purely decorative feature. An embrasured parapet neatly terminates the tower walls. The pyramid roof was rebuilt during the restoration by the Countess of Dunmore, as was also the roof of the main part of the building. We cannot be sure what form the original tower roof took, but an ancient song from North Uist: '*Latha Ceann na Traghad*' – Battle of the Strand, around 1500 – tells of '*Tur maol na raigeach manach*' – blunt tower of the tonsured monks. This song provides further evidence as to its existence prior to the time of Alasdair Crotach, and also describes the monks who occupied the priory up to the time of the Reformation.

A beggar's badge, made of lead, features the tower with a pointed roof,

The 'Gothic' style window set in the east gable, wrought from local amphibolite, is one of the finest external features.

so we can be almost certain that this was its form, at least since the restoration in 1787 by Captain Alexander Macleod.

We have on record in the *Statistical Account* of 1792, for the parish of Harris, by the Revd John Macleod, Scarista, that there were at that time no fewer than seventy-five poor persons in the parish, who were dependant on others better off for the necessities or comforts of life. These poor people were given marks or badges to identify them from less deserving vagabonds. J. Balfour Paul, writing on beggars' badges, quotes: 'and if any were found begging without a token, be it a man to be strucken throw the hand, and be it a woman to brunt on the cheik and banest the toun, but favoures.' The cheek of a woman and the hand of a man were naturally considered to be the parts which transgressors would least willingly have disfigured or maimed.

The impression of St. Clement's church on the badge is possibly the earliest, though not a wholly accurate, portrayal of the church. It also features a bull's head – symbol of the Macleods – and the inscription: 'Roudil St. Clements'.

The present church roof of heavy slates on timber sarking, supported by strong wooden trusses, was put on around 1873 by the Countess of Dunmore, who had taken a personal interest in the derelict church; and though she carried out a complete repair of the building, sadly, the interior was not completed or furnished in any way, and to this day it remains an empty shell – a church of memories only.

Prior to this, and having been roofless for a period of time, it was used by fishermen for repairing and tanning their herring nets. This was years after the herring fishery which was being developed by Captain Alexander Macleod in 1779, and there was still a remnant of the fishing being pursued. The natural fibre nets of that time had to be regularly treated with a preservative called cutch. This was a preparation of tannin obtained from the bark of japonica and acacia wood, mainly produced in Burma, and was used in the manufacture of nets and twine, the process being repeated at various times throughout the life of the nets. The roofless, derelict building provided a workplace where large vats could be heated on open fires; the nets then tanned were hung to dry on beams placed across the walls. Canvas sails and the rigging of boats could be treated in the same manner. This may well have been the only time in its whole history that the church was ever in daily use – albeit for secular purposes.

The various sculptures that adorn the outer walls of the tower are: On the north wall, a bull's head (Macleod emblem). On the south wall is a panel portraying a naked female, holding a child. In the centre of the east

The south wall of the tower.

The Beggar's Badge, depicting St. Clement's church and the Macleod emblem.
© *The Trustees of the National Museums of Scotland, 1993.*

wall, just above the main ridge, is a carving said to represent two fishermen in a boat, though in its present eroded condition, one could not say
with any degree of certainty what it looked like originally. Immediately
below this is the figure of a horse. On the west wall is a canopied niche,
containing an effigy of St. Clement. Below this, there are two interesting
figures, placed in a canted position; the one on the left is clothed in
'Highland dress' and to the right of him is the other, wearing a jacket of
jerkin, and 'possibly' tight fitting trunks or hose. This figure is known
locally as *dealbh na leisge* – the picture of laziness. He is said to have

been, for centuries, holding the symbol of his manhood in both hands – until the Countess of Dunmore, offended by its rude appearance, ordered her ghillie to shoot it off. An excellent marksman, he neatly amputated the protruding part. Another panel depicting the crucifixion is situated above the main entrance to the church, in the north wall of the building.

Inside, the church is not furnished in any way, and no trace of the original woodwork remains; but the richly carved stonework compensates for the otherwise bare interior. The internal walls of random-laid stone were, at one time, smooth plastered – traces of this can be seen on the stonework – and probably finished in white, giving a totally different look and feeling to the rather stark appearance of the walls today. The arched entrances to the cross aisles, or transepts, differ in shape and material. The northern arch is built from black amphibolite and is of semi-circular shape, while the southern arch is pointed, and built from sandstone, which has eroded considerably. The carved detail on both arches is similar, and looks like having been the best feature of the internal stonework. T.S. Muir, in the *Ecclesiastical Architecture of Scotland* states that the chapels, or transepts, were not built before the fifteenth century. Exactly when cannot be certain.

The tower is entered through a door in the west end of the nave, and up a narrow stair built into the wall of the tower, leading to the first floor level. There is also an entrance from outside at this level, as the ground rises steeply here, against the west wall. A window in the east wall at one time looked into the nave, but is now built up. From here the stone stair leads to the next floor level. Wooden ladders take you up another two floors, with a final ladder that leads to a hatch in the roof of the tower, opening out onto the parapet. This position (no longer accessible to the public) affords a commanding view over the Minch and the Sound of Harris.

6

Alasdair Crotach's Tomb

Alasdair Crotach's tomb is recognised as one of the finest in Scotland, and I can do no better than to quote the excellent description from the 1928 report of the Royal Commission on Ancient and Historical Monuments and Constructions of Scotland:

Ten feet long and recessed 1 foot 4½ inches within the wall, it has a semicircular arch of sculptured freestone panels relieved by plain schist bands. The moulded label is of schist and is roughly triangular; it terminates in moulded stops. Label and soffit are enriched with nailheads. The back of the recess is of freestone and contains sculptured panels.

The panels on the arch are nine in number, there being four on each side of that forming the keystone, on which is carved the Saviour on a cross upheld by a seated figure of the Father in pontifical robes and tiara. Some details are rather worn but are described by Mr. J.S. Richardson thus: above the dexter shoulder of this crowned figure is a bird for St John, over the sinister shoulder an angel for St Matthew; under the right foot of the father is a winged ox for St Luke, and under the left foot the winged lion of St Mark, of whose name some letters appear on the scroll. The figure on the cross has the arms straight and the head inclined to the dexter. The body is emaciated and clothed only in a loin cloth; the legs are crossed below the knees.

Of the panels on the dexter side first at the foot shows two figures; that to the dexter, with an axe (?) as symbol, may represent St Mathias. The second shows one figure bearing a St Andrew's cross, which may thus stand for that apostle; while on

The tomb of Alasdair Crotach: Alexander Macleod, 8th chief of the Macleods of Dunvegan and Harris.

the scroll as it crosses the companion may be discerned what are the opening letters of the name Mat(thew). The third panel is occupied by an angel swinging a censer. In the fourth the more complete figure is the only one in the whole assemblage which is without a beard; in the right hand is a sword or rod; the figure may stand for the youthful St John. To his companion there is no certain clue; he may be St Peter.

On the sinister side the first panel from the top shows a figure holding a cross staff, and with a shell on his halo, while on the scroll are the letters S JACOBI for James the Greater. The other personage offers no mark of identification. The second panel in this order, corresponding to that on the dexter side, has an angel with censer. In the next division below, the figures face each other, the only case in which they do so, that to the left also pointing upwards or in the direction of the crucifixion panel. On the scroll held by the left hand may be read SCI BARTHOL, for St Bartholomew; while on the part held by the companion figure are the letters S THOM(A) for St Thomas. This dramatic confrontation of the figures suggests an illustration of the one apostle convincing his doubting brother. Of the pair of figures in the last panel, the scroll again names one as JACOBI, presumably James the Less; while his companion bears what may be a chalice, which is suggestive of St John, only that the figure shows a beard. The title below is illegible, but St John would not occur twice.

All the figures with the exception noted, have long hair, beard and unshaven upper lip. Each is dressed in the quilted coat of the west, with a mantle and tippet over, and wears a halo. As they number just twelve, and some at least can be identified as apostles, the likelihood is that as a whole they represent these.

The space at the back of the recess is occupied by three horizontal rows of panels above a plain base. On the top line are three panels. In the centre an angel blows a curved trumpet on either side of a blazing sun or star of twelve rays, alternately straight and curved. In each of the panels flanking this device is an angel holding an upright candle.

The middle row begins at the dexter end with a castle, having a great tower and a smaller one showing an entrance. The stepped character of the battlements is rather Irish than Scottish. The next panel shows a bishop with mitre and crook in the attitude of blessing. The central of the five panels displays the Blessed Virgin

St. Clement: as depicted on Alasdair Crotach's tomb.

with Child; she sits crowned on a throne within a decorated canopy, and holds a lily (?) in her right hand. Next to her is the figure named on its base as (-) CE CLEMENT, i.e. St Clement, dressed in episcopal vestments, with mitre and crook, and holding in his right hand a skull. The final panel on this level shows a galley under sail; this feature, like the castle on the corresponding panel at the other end, being part of the Macleod arms.

The bottom row shows first a hunting scene, as illustrated; next a representation of Michael and Satan at the weighing of souls; and thirdly a finely cut Latin inscription as follows –

HIC LOCULUS CO(M)POSUIT
P(E) D(OMI)N(U)M ALLEXA(N)DER FILIUS VIL(EL)MI
MAC CLOD D(OMI)NO DE DU(N)VEGAN
ANNO D(OMI)NI M CCCCC XXVIII

The letters omitted or indicated by a sign are shown in brackets.

It is obvious that there has been no effort to secure grammatical agreement in the words, but the sense can be made out to the effect that the tomb was prepared by Alexander Macleod of Dunvegan, son of William Macleod, that is by Alasdair Crotach, who was dead before 1547. The same Alasdair was responsible for some of the building at Dunvegan Castle.

The figure on the tomb is attired in armour of plate with ornamented bascinet and camail, while a scalloped edge of mail appears below the body plates. The shoes are round-toed sabbatons and rest upon a crocodile or other lizard. The sword is held by hilt and quillion perpendicularily between the legs, and has straight quillions with trefoiled ends and a pear shaped pommel. There is a richly-ornamented hip belt. The armour is thus a mixture of old and new fashions. At the head and foot of the projecting part of the tomb is a lion, that by the head being much wasted.

Another tomb in the same south wall tends to be overlooked in favour of Alasdair Crotach's more elaborate edifice, but this one, to me, represents a higher order of craftsmanship. It is described in the same 1928 Royal Commission report thus:

A second tomb lies immediately west of the transept; the recess, 6½ feet long and 1 foot deep, is contained within a semicircular arch with triangular label, surmounted by a trefoil; the arch mouldings terminate in miniature bases similar in type to those on the transept arches. The tympanum between label and arch encloses a panel depicting the crucifixion with Mary and John; the Christ here with straight arms and with the feet crossed, wearing a loincloth. The recess, which has an illegible inscription in Gothic lettering wrought on the back, contains an effigy clad in armour with pointed helm, wearing a hauberk under robe and hood. The feet, clad in sabbatons, rest on two intertwined hounds, and there is a hound on either side of the head. On the chest and lying between the legs is a sword with depressed quillions and onion shaped pommel, grasped in the left hand by the hilt and in the right by the pommel. At the left side is a dagger.

This tomb has been more accurately constructed and with a much better finish to the carved stonework. It is simple in design, yet strong and graceful: quietly adorned and totally worked in amphibolite. Some earlier writers have suggested that carved sandstone panels – similar to those on Alasdair Crotach's tomb – had been removed from the recess. This is not so, the original panels are still there, five in number, carved from black schist, but eroded and worn to the extent that very little remains that is legible. This is possibly due to having been closer to the centre of the fire that gutted the building in 1784. Part of the Gothic lettering on one of the panels shows the last five letters of the word (comp)OSUIT; a similar word appears on the tomb of Alasdair Crotach and means 'prepared'. A date, 1539, is recorded in *Late Mediaeval Munumental Sculpture in the West Highlands* by K.A. Steer and J.W.M. Bannerman, who assume the tomb to be that of William, son and successor to Alexander Macleod (Alasdair Crotach).

The inscription, partly legible at the time of their report, reads:

hi[c.e]st.loculu[s.co(m)p]osuit p(er)/.
d(omi)n(u)[m].../ [a]nno.d(omi)ni.m[.cccc]c.
xx[xi]x

translated thus:

This is the tomb prepared by Lord . . .
in the year of our Lord 1539.

William Macleod died in September 1551, less than five years after his father. He had married Agnes, daughter of Hugh Fraser of Lovat, in 1540, for which deed he was granted suitable lands. Further land was added to his possessions by crown charter in 1542, when Trotternish and Sleat in Skye, along with North Uist, were attached to his inheritance of Harris and Dunvegan. They had one daughter, Mary, who in 1553 married George, Earl of Huntly.

William was succeeded by a close relative, John Macleod of Minginish – *Ian a' Chuil Bhain* – (John of the fair locks) who, on his death, was also laid to rest in Rodil. John Macleod's daughter married Malcolm Campbell of Strond, and their son, Kenneth Campbell, was married to Anne, daughter of Donald Macleod of Berneray.

7

Roderick of the Blades

A third tomb with a carved effigy, which was at one time situated in the south transept, is now located in the north-west corner of the nave, close to the entrance. A figure in plate armour with carved lions at head and feet, and with a sword similar to that on the tomb of (William Macleod), is carved from black amphibolite. This is possibly the tomb of John Macleod of Minginish; there is no inscription or date, so here we must rely on oral tradition.

Local folklore tells of tombs being re-used for later burials, as was certainly the case with at least one of the tombs in the floor of the nave, where an iron grating was fixed below the stone slab – to allow the remains to be shaken through, before another body was interred. This is said to have been the burial place of the Macleod standard bearers and pipers.

The last person reputedly buried in the tomb of John Macleod was *Ruairidh na Lann* (Roderick of the Blades), so named because of his fame as a swordsman. His skill no doubt encouraged him to go to the rescue of his wife from *Long nan Daoine*, the ship *William* of Donaghadee, near Belfast, which in November 1739, on the order of Sir Alexander Macdonald of Sleat and his brother-in-law Norman Macleod of Harris – in their scheme to clear certain areas and deport the unfortunate tenants to be sold as slaves to the American plantations. This was a common and lucrative trade at the time, in which the ship *William* was involved for most of her trading life. There is record of a voyage to America in 1766, when she carried a similar cargo from Newry in Northern Ireland to Boston. She was described then as one of the better ships of the time. She was designed for carrying cargo, but with only a maximum height of 4 feet 9 inches between the decks, only children could stand upright.

The pierced cross that terminates the east gable, with the tower behind.

The vessel, which was registered in Liverpool, was chartered by Norman Macleod of Berneray – acting as agent on behalf of Messrs Macdonald and Macleod – and he himself was to sail as supercargo, as part of his reward in the deal. After loading some men, women and children at Lochportain in North Uist, the *William* sailed to Harris and anchored in Finsbay. Having chosen a day when they knew the ablebodied men were out on the moor, rounding up sheep, they came ashore and crossed to the west side of the island to take women and children from their homes. On returning home that evening, Ruairidh na Lann discovered that his wife, along with the rest of the women and children of the small settlement of Strangragarry, situated about halfway between Northton and Scarista, had been taken.

It was known that the ship was still at Finsbay, sheltering for the night before sailing to Loch Bracadale in Skye, where more 'cargo' was waiting to be loaded – making a total of one hundred and eleven in all. Ruairidh, armed with his claymore, made for Finsbay: a perilous journey in the dark, of about seven miles over bog and moor, and having to skirt round several lochs on the way. He took a rowing boat at Finsbay, and in the dark, boarded the *William*. Having securely barred the doors to the crew's quarters, he opened a hatch. Calling to his wife, he reached down and pulled her up to the deck, and thence to home and safety.

After a stormy passage through the Minch, during which several of the captives were put ashore on the islands of Rhum and Jura because of ill health, and also some of the children who were considered to be too young, the *William* was forced to put into Donaghadee for urgent repairs, before proceeding further on its long voyage. Here the captives were helped to escape from the two barns in which they had been held. All ninety-six of them were later rounded up and taken before the magistrates at Donaghadee, to be tried for escaping from captivity (the master and owner of the *William* had claimed them to be 'felons, who had escaped from a ship on passage from the Highlands of Scotland to America'). When the real story of their miserable and helpless condition became known, they were released unconditionally. Most of them found local employment, and eventually some returned to Harris, while others settled in Ireland. The master of the *William* and his accomplice, Norman Macleod, fled the country after a warrant had been issued for their arrest. The real perpetrators of the crime, Messrs Macdonald and Macleod, though strongly suspected, and under the threat of imminent prosecution, escaped justice. There is a strong belief that a deal was forged between them and Duncan Forbes of Culloden – the Lord President of the Court of Session – which later came to light at the time of the '45 rising, when they were found on the side of the Government.

There are to this day, a number of *Ruairidh na Lann's* descendants living in South Harris; but there is no trace now of the settlement at Strangragarry, or *Stangaidhgearraidh* as it is known in Gaelic: only the vague outline of enclosure dykes on the hillside above the road. The ruin of the neighbouring settlement of Nisisidh, can still be seen beside the road. The bardess, Mairi *Nighean Alasdair Ruaidh*, is said to have lived here for some time; and it is more than likely to have been her birthplace.

One old woman who was present at the funeral of *Ruairidh na Lann*, claimed he was the fourteenth to have been buried in that same tomb.

8

Stones

Placed in an upright position against a wall in the north transept are five grave-slabs which were lifted from the floor of the church, during routine repair and maintenance work, to preserve and protect them from further wear. All but one of them has a carved sword, surrounded by scrolls and various other ornamentation. Two of the stones are believed to be pre-1500, which places them at least thirty years, and possibly much more, before the time of the restoration by Alasdair Crotach. The remaining stone is totally different in design, dated 1725, and bearing the letters R C, A M S ; it also has carvings said to represent Masonic symbols but which are more likely to be marks associated with the particular sculptor, or marks generally used by the craft of undertaker and monumental sculptor – in the absence of any other instructions, they would embellish a stone with their own mark or ornamentation. These marks appear on two other tombs outside the church. One set is on the grave of Donald Macleod of Berneray – the marble plaque commemorating his death appears to have been built into an older *caibeal* or burial chapel, which has an earlier plaque, surrounded by those marks, but has no legible lettering. However, if the marks coincide with those on the other tombs, dated 1725 and 1738 respectively, then this tomb would predate Donald Macleod's burial by approximately fifty to sixty years. The other tomb with similar marks is that of William Macleod who died in 1738, eldest son of Sir Norman Macleod of Berneray. Sir Norman's father, *Ruairidh Mor* – Sir Roderick Macleod – was fifteenth chief of Macleod: a great scholar who wrote in both Gaelic and Latin, but who did not understand a word of English.

    The carvings on the three graves are similar, and depict: a skull; crossed bones; coffin; hour-glass; various tools including a mallet and stone carving chisels; bell; and spade.

One of the five grave slabs from the floor of the church, dated 1725, with 'mason marks' clockwise from the top left: coffin; skull; hour-glass; gravedigger's tools; bell; and crossed bones.

The disc-headed cross, mounted in a south window. The original location of this stone is not known.

Certain marks were frequently used (though usually more discreetly) by travelling masons and other tradesmen, to identify them as genuine craftsmen, thus affording them a degree of protection from imposters who would turn out cheaper work of inferior quality – this was the original and true purpose of Freemasonry.

Mounted on a window-sill in the south wall is a stone in the form of a disc-headed cross; it bears a representation of the crucifixion on one side and, on the reverse, is decorated with an intertwining pattern. The original location of this stone is not known, as it was found lying outside the church. The lower end has possibly been shortened or else it was broken. It is now set into a plinth on the window-sill.

An irregularily shaped stone basin, or mortar, sits by the tower entrance; its use is uncertain. Had it been a font, then it would have been more accurately shaped and embellished. It is more likely to have been used for the pounding of grain, or for the preparation of shellfish – a regular part of the island monk's diet.

One other interesting piece of sculpture that tends to be unnoticed is situated on the eastern apex of the church roof. It is a carved stone cross of pierced form, that neatly terminates the gable.

Of the missing inscription panels in some of the outside burial chapels, there is no sign; possibly they were broken or else removed and 're-cycled'! It has been suggested that the 'RC, AMS' stone was one of those removed from a *caibeal*, but this is not so, as the stone inside the church is of totally different dimensions.

Outside the churchyard enclosure wall there is a line of boulders extending in a southerly direction, from the south-west corner. This, presumably, was a boundary wall at one time, and possibly an agricultural or livestock fold, further reinforcing the idea of long-term occupation by the Augustinian monks.

9

West Highland *Birlinn*

The vessel depicted on one of the carved panels set in the back of the tomb of Alasdair Crotach is possibly the finest illustration in existence of a West Highland *birlinn*. The design evolved from the longships of the Viking invaders; the high prow and stern-post that proudly accentuates the sheerline is typical of the Norse vessels. A single central mast with a square sail was the main means of propulsion. Provision was made for seventeen pairs of oars, which could be used when conditions were suitable, and for manoeuvring in restricted waters. The only marked difference between this *birlinn* and the Viking longships is the rudder; in this case it was mounted directly to the stern-post, whereas the longships had a side-mounted rudder or 'steerboard' from which comes the nautical term – starboard. The rudder on the Rodil *birlinn* is mounted with iron pintles and gudgeons – a method that remains unchanged on many boats to this day.

The *birlinn* was approximately seventy-five feet in length, and a crew of about forty men would be required to man fully a vessel of this size. It is comparable in size with the Viking ship – of the *karfi* type – which was excavated from a farm at Gokstad, Norway, in 1880 and which is now preserved in the Viking Ship Hall at Bygdoy. It is 23.24 metres in length, and 5.2 metres in breadth, with provision for sixteen pairs of oars. The *karfi* were not as large as the sea-going longships, but were meant for coastal use. Yet they were capable of long voyages, for in 1893, an exact replica of this vessel was sailed across the Atlantic Ocean to be displayed at the World Exhibition in Chicago.

Like all the other tomb carvings, the Rodil *birlinn* is very finely and accurately detailed, even to the stitching in the sail. The slotted oar-ports are shown, which allow the oars, on account of their length, to be shipped from inboard. These oar-ports could be shuttered, when under sail, to prevent water from entering.

The *birlinn*, mainly used for the personal transport of the chief, were also, like their predecessors, raiding or fighting ships – even piracy was considered to be a sport to be pursued at every opportunity. But there was also a nobler duty assigned to them; a crown charter of 1498, granting lands in Skye and Harris to the Macleods, states as one of its terms, that they were obliged to keep one ship of twenty-six oars and two of sixteen oars each, for the service of the King in peace and war.

The restored Gokstad ship, in the Viking Ship Hall at Bygdoy.

The birlinn or galley, carved on the tomb of Alasdair Crotach, bears a strong resemblance to the Viking longships.

These boats portray a romantic image in ancient songs and stories, but for the men who had to spend long, arduous hours and days at the oars, exposed to wind and spray, it must have been physically wearying and extremely hazardous. Yet to be a crewman on the chief's *birlinn* in those days, must have been a prestigious position. On long voyages, their diet would have mainly consisted of meal and water; but there was one item of 'convenience food' that was still used by fishermen at the beginning of this century. A form of pudding, known as *marag-dheochdaidh* is made from a mixture of oatmeal and fish livers, packed into part of a sheep's intestine, and secured with a knot at each end. This was not cooked, but was sat on in the boat; best results were obtained when rowing, the heat generated working on the ingredients to produce a semi-liquid which could be sucked from a small hole when required. Definitely not for the refined tastes of today's mariners!

10

Once Upon a Time

During the time that nearby Rodil House was still in use as a private residence, a party of young guests who were enjoying an evening of merriment placed a wager as to which of them would be bold enough to enter the Church of St. Clements's in the dead of the night – and return to the house, with a bone from one of the tombs as evidence of having done so.

On accepting the challenge, one of the young men, whose reward was to be a brand new bonnet, went out all alone in the dark night, heading for the church. After some considerable time had passed, whilst still more bets were being placed on his success, he returned to Rodil House with a human skull. The promise of a fine new bonnet was his.

Entering the church later that night to replace the skull in its rightful resting place, he was conscious of the eerie presence of other people round about him – watching the safe return of their absent fellow from the past. As time went on, more and more were gathering around him. Eventually, with his grim task completed, the young man had to struggle and push his way out through the dense mass of 'generations past' that were blocking his exit.

Full of terror, and sadly regretting his earlier boldness, which now had left him weakened and helpless, physically and mentally destroyed, he made his way back to Rodil House, where he remained in that sorry state till the end of his days.

Norman Jr. Macmillan, retired crofter and coastguard, has lived all his life at Rodil, within a hundred yards of St. Clement's. Norman gave me the story of the young men from Rodil House who took the skull from the tomb.

11

Son of a Thief

A notorious family of raiders, descended from the Macleods of Harris, had for some time, control over the northern part of the island. They were *Clann Mhic Iain*, grandsons of John Macleod, plundering where they could, taking sheep and cattle or whatever they could lay their hands on. Once, on a raid of the west side, they used as a temporary home the church in Scarista. When Macleod of Rodil heard of their presence, he sent some of his men to secure them. Not only did they do that, but they also set fire to the church. Only one of the brothers and a young boy escaped being burned alive.

Another time, an old woman who had suffered from their raiding, heard that the brothers were near. She killed and skinned two cats, and set them in a pot on the fire. Leaving the house, she watched them enter, take the pot, and consume the entire contents with great satisfaction.

Some years after, one of the brothers, *Ian Mor*, had died and was buried at Rodil. The old woman borrowed an iron 'still' from the Laird's house, and set it on a fire in the graveyard. When the water was briskly boiling she tipped it all over *Ian Mor*'s grave, whilst reciting this verse –

> *Mhic mearlach nan laogh 's nan gobhar,*
> *Mise gu h-ard 's thusa fodham;*
> *Tha thu shios gu domhain, domhain,*
> *Is dortaidh mi' se seo mu 'd ghobhall.*

> Son of a thief of calves and goats,
> I am above and you below me;
> You are down deeply, deeply,
> I will pour this in your lap.

12

From Rodil to Rome

In the ninth century, when the Western Isles were being invaded by the Norsemen, the fear of valuable artefacts from various religious locations being stolen or destroyed, led to some of the more precious items being shipped to Rome for safe keeping.

This must have been a massive operation, involving a large fleet of vessels, to ensure a safe passage and protection from the Vikings or indeed any other pirate vessels. The scale of such an operation gives some idea as to the great value of the relics gathered from the west coast and island sites.

Relics from the priory at Rodil were taken and, along with the rest, were shipped to the basilica of San Clemente in Rome, where they remained for about two hundred years, before being moved to the great Benedictine Abbey of Cava, near Salerno.

With only a vague hope of ever being able to find out something of their whereabouts – considering that over a thousand years had passed since their removal from Rodil – I wrote to the Abbey at Cava, not even knowing for sure if that place did indeed exist. Two or three months went by without any response, so I decided to try one more way of making contact. I wrote, this time, to St. Andrew's Church of Scotland in Rome, and very soon had a reply from Revd David F. Huie, who confirmed that the Benedictine Abbey of La Trinita di Cava, which was built around 1011–1025 still stands, and is one of the most important centres for the study of medieval history in Southern Italy, possessing valuable archives, as well as a museum.

Revd Huie enlisted the help of his Session Clerk, Sig. Guiseppe Caruso, who is also headmaster of a school in Rome, to try to contact the Abbey at Cava. A telephone call was all that was necessary to reach the Director of

donatus fuit, ac solenni et honorifico funere in Cavensi Ecclesia Sanctuarii, ante Altare maius Tumulo reconditus huiusmo-
di inscriptione notat. ✠ Hic iacet Corpus Abbatis Leonis Secundi,
cuius Anima cum Sanctis gaudeat in fine mundi. ✠

Hi sunt Cavensis Monasterii Primi Duodecim Sanctissimi Institu-
tores ac Patres; Hi Columnae duodecim quibus Cavensis Domus
ingens moles innititur et fulcitur; Hi Cavensis Thesauri praeci-
puae margaritae; Hi pretiosi lapides vivi in caelestis aedificii stru-
cturam per superni Artificis manum aptati atque dispositi. Quo-
rum nos hoc in loco non laudes et gloriam verbis nostris explica-
re (quod valde longum ac difficile esset) intendimus; sed bre-
vitatem tantum compendiose ac breviter seriem describere Reliquiarum, quae in Cavensi sacrario congruo honore servantur.

Series Sacrarum Reliquiarum quae in Caven. Mon. Ecclesia et sacrario
asservantur.

✠ De Ligno s. Crucis Dominicae.
  Spina sacra Coronae Dominicae.
  De Capillis B. V. Matris Mariae
✠ De Veste eiusdem.
  Dens s. Joannis Baptistae.
  De capillis eiusdem.
  Caput s. Felicitatis Mar. Mat. 7 fil. m.
  Brachium s. Simeonis.
  Brachium s. Adiutoris mart.
  Brachium s. Jac. minor. Apost.
  De Relig. eiusdem.
  De Capite s. Bartholomei Apost.
  De Relig. ss. Petri et Pauli Apost.
  De Relig. s. Jacobi maioris Apost.
  De Relig. s. Philippi Apost.
  De Relig. s. Simonis Apost.
  De Relig. s. Thadei Apost.
  De Relig. s. Marci Euangel.
✠ De Costa s. Mariae Magdal.
✠ De Rel. eiusdem.
✠ De Brachio s. Annae matris Virg. Mar.
  De Capite, Costa, et Sang. ss. Placidi et soc.
  De Omnibus, Carne, et carbon. s. Laur. mar.
✠ De Maxilla s. Sebastiani Mart.

✠ De Cruce et Relig. s. Blasii mart.
  De Costa et Relig. s. Georgii Mart.
  De Brachio et Relig. s. Cornelii Pa. et Mar.
✠ De Brachio s. Vincentii Mart.
  De Relig. s. Stephani pro. mart.
  De Relig. ss. Innocentium.
  De Relig. s. Januarii Ep. et Mart.
✠ De Relig. s. Alexandri Papae et Mart.
  De Relig. s. Mercurii Mart.
  De Relig. ss. Cosmae et Damiani Mart.
  De Relig. s. Donati Ep. et Mart.
  De Relig. s. Sixti Papae et Mart.
  De Relig. s. Clementis Papae et Mart.
  De Relig. s. Getulii Mart. et mart.
  De Relig. ss. Quatuor Coronatorum
  De Relig. s. Nerei Mart.
  De Relig. s. Theodori Mart.
  De Relig. s. Chrysogoni Mart.
  De Relig. s. Nazarii Mart.
  De Rel. ss. Tiburtii, Valer. et Max. Mar.
  De Relig. ss. Duodecim fratrum Mart.
✠ De Relig. s. Cypriani Ep. et Mart.
  De Relig. s. Eustachii Mart.
  De Rel. ss. Ciriaci, Largi, et Smaragd. Mar.

*Page from the manuscript of Abbot Alessandro Ridolfi, 1528, recording ancient relics held
at the Benedictine Abbey of Cava.*

MODULARIO
Beni L.I.C. - 2/B

MOD. B

Badia di Cava   8. IV   19 91

Ministero per i Beni Culturali
e Ambientali

BIBLIOTECA DEL MONUMENTO NAZIONALE
84010 BADIA DI CAVA (Salerno)

Al Sig. Giuseppe Caruso
Via San Sosti, 33
00132 - ROMA

Prot. N° 96/15

Risposta al f. del
N.°

Óggetto: reliquia di S. Clemente.

      Facendo seguito ai contatti telefonici
intercorsi, Le comunico che la reliquia di
S. Clemente è ancora indicata in un elenco
contenuto nel manoscritto inedito dell'Abate
Alessandro Ridolfi:"Historia Sacri Monasterii
Cavensis", anno 1582 (v. copia fotostatica
allegata); detta reliquia, però, non si con-
serva più in questo monastero.

      Sperando di essermi reso utile, Le
porgo distinti saluti.

IL DIRETTORE
(D. Eugenio Andrea Gargiulo)

Letter from the Director of the library at Cava.

the Abbey library, who is also a parish priest. A few days later, I had a letter along with a page photocopied from a previously unpublished manuscript, written by Abbot Alessandro Ridolfi in 1582, which catalogues the relics that were held by the Abbey of Cava at that time.

Sig. Caruso's reply from Cava, translated, reads:

> Following our telephone contacts, I have to inform you that the relics of San Clemente are still recorded in a list contained in an unpublished manuscript of Abbot Alessandro Ridolfi *A History of the Holy Monastery of Cava*, dated 1582 (see attached photocopy); the relics mentioned, however, are no longer kept at this monastery. Hoping to have been of some use, I extend greetings.
>
> Il Direttore
> D. Eugenio Andrea Gargiulo.

What those relics were, and where they now are, is still unknown; and maybe, better left undisturbed. Guiseppe Caruso has since visited me, and of course St. Clement's church, on a holiday to Scotland. I am also grateful to him for a book, describing the Abbey of La Trinita di Cava.

13

St. Clements at the Present Time

St. Clement's church today is in the care of Historic Buildings and Monuments – more recently called Historic Scotland – who are responsible for all care and maintenance. The building is in an excellent state of repair; open to the public at all times (entry is free, but there is a box for local charities inside) it is well worth a visit, to share in feelings of the past.

An agreement was drawn up on 27th April 1912, between The Right Honourable Alexander Edward Murray, Earl of Dunmore VC, MVC and The Commissioners of His Majesty's Works and Public Buildings, to become the Guardians of Rodil Priory Church. Part of the agreement states that the Earl of Dunmore is not to support any application for religious services and that the church is not to be used for ecclesiastical purposes except on the occasion of funerals.

Title to the property remains with the Dunmore family.